Praise

It has been said that the
The second best time is today. Through their book, *A Life Well Lived*,
the challenge presented by the Barine brothers is clear: our life's purpose
should not be to leave a monument to ourselves but rather to leave a legacy
for others.

Too many people live their lives for themselves and they have planted
no trees under which others might enjoy shade. A selfish life is in the end a
wasted life. However, a life lived with the purpose of helping others is a life
that will be remembered and affirmed long after one has finished his or her
time on earth. The Bible declares, *"We have this treasure in earthen vessels"*
(2 Cor. 4:7). Even after the vessel has perished, the treasure shoulddendure.
That is the legacy of a life well lived.

Dr. James J. Seymour – *Accumulated Resources,*
North Carolina, USA

This book will compel you to live today with tomorrow in mind. After
reading it, you will want to live your life differently, and I'm sure that is
what Kirimi and Stephen Barine had in mind – for you to live a life that is
noteworthy!

David Kadalie
Youth for Christ Regional Director, East Indian Island Nations.
Cape Town, South Africa

We all seem so busy, piling activity upon activity. But are we doing
things that make a lasting difference? I commend this timely book, *A
Life Well Lived: Living to Leave a Legacy*, by Kirimi and Stephen Barine.

Not only do the authors call us to invest in other people's lives and our relationship with God, they also offer helpful guidance on how to do it. From my personal experience with the authors, I know they practice what they preach.

John Maust
President, Media Associates International
Chicago, USA

I believe every one that has been touched by God has a desire for a life that will not just be summed up by two dates separated by a hyphen inscribed on a gravestone. There should be a compelling urge to leave a lovely legacy in this world, but many don't know how to be intentional about it.

In this much-needed book, my good friend Kirimi and his brother Stephen have given us unique insights and practical guide to help us live not only destiny fulfilling but also legacy-minded lives. I highly recommended their brilliant work.

Through his integrity, leadership and writing, Kirimi is a powerful voice of influence not only in Kenya but in many other parts of the African continent and the world at large.

Bishop Jovie Galaraga,
Director for Philippines and Asia, Harvest Time International
Chairman, International Bible Society Philippines
Publisher, Charis Communications
Manila, Philippines

Kirimi and Stephen Barine have produced a trailblazer that no doubt poses very relevant questions to every living human being. They are unequivocally asking us if we are leaving footprints on the sands of time. After reading this book, you cannot escape being motivated to live in such a way as to leave a legacy. They have proved that living well can be measured in terms of leaving a legacy. I strongly recommend this book to all.

Apostle Dr. Frederick Nwosu, Ph.D., D.D.
Presiding Bishop of First Pentecostal Power Ministries
Chancellor and founder Emmanuel University
Author – KNOWING HIM (In a Broad Spectrum of Leadership Perspectives)
North Carolina, U.S.A.

A.K Barine has done it again! After *Rediscovering Leadership*, a book that has transformed lives of many people in different organizations and countries, Kirimi has now teamed up with his brother Stephen to write on living to leave a legacy. This book, *A life well lived* sets forth the reasons we must leave a legacy and how we can do it. For anyone who wants to live a life with a purpose, this is a must read.

Patrick Muriithi Nyaga
Pastor & Author of Called to Serve – The Spirit of Sacrificial Servanthood
Nairobi, Kenya

We are in this world with a purpose, and it's normal to ask the following questions: What will I be remembered for? What would I like written on my tombstone?

Among other things, *A Life Well Lived: Living to Leave a legacy* challenges the Christian and non-Christian on the need to place a high value on one's relationship with God and with other people. The author also analyses the life of Jesus, the perfect example of purposeful living, for ease of emulation. This is what makes the book necessary reading for those who wish to leave a lasting mark once they are ought of the scene.

Chinedum E. Isiguzo
Missionary & Bible Teacher
Lagos, Nigeria

Every believer ought to recognize that they have a purpose in life and pursue it relentlessly if they are to have a lasting legacy. And this is made possible through strong interpersonal relationships.

Moreover, with God's help it is possible for every Christian to live in such a way that he or she impacts those whom they relate with. This is what the Barines so eloquently prove in their writing.

I strongly endorse this book and pray that all who read it will be open to it's message so that their lives count now and after they have gone to heaven.

Dr. Armstrong Cheggeh
Presiding Bishop, Fountain of Life Churches
Kentucky, U.S.A.

The Barines have hit the bulls' eye on many voices. It is good to hear one that is speaking through the fog and zeroing in like laser on the core foundations of Christian living, The book needs to be read and reread to keep us all on the target.

Dr. Mike Garrett L.P.C.
Teaching Pastor
Licensed Professional Counselor
Crossroads Fellowship Church
North Carolina, USA

A Life Well Lived

Living to Leave a Legacy

Kirimi Barine
&
Stephen Barine

A Life Well Lived: Living to Leave a Legacy

Published by:

Integrity Publishers Inc.
P.O. Box 789,
Wake Forest, NC 27588
U.S.A.
info@integritypublishers.org

ISBN 13: 978-0-9821175-2-1

ISBN 10: 0-9821175-2-3

Cover Photo Credits:

Printed in the United States of America

Dedication

Dedicated to our late dad, Rev. Phinehas Barine Murungi, who went to be with the Lord in October, 1998 after he had served the Lord with dedication for as long as we can remember. By his example, we were inspired to trust the Lord and depend upon Him for our provision, and also to serve other people as a ministry to the Lord.

The way our dad served the Lord in his generation left not only a lasting legacy but also a challenge for us all.

Acknowledgements

Writing a book is not the effort of the author(s) alone.

In our case, our families have provided material support and, even more important, the encouragement that it can be done. Without their prayers and emotional support, it would have been difficult even to put the ideas together.

Although it is not possible to mention them by name individually, the church families and friends whom we fellowship with have also made remarkable contribution in the realization of this book.

Hardly any long write-up is without a misplaced comma here or a missing full-stop there. We thank Wilson Macharia and Esther Nyaga who, in an effort to reduce such mistakes, read through the manuscript, seeking clarification from us where they thought necessary.

But the Person we feel indebted to most is Jesus Christ, who is not only our Lord and Saviour, but also our all in all. Had he not come into this world, become the benchmark of a life well lived, and then died for us on the cross, we would be nothing and even the theme of this book would not exist.

Contents

Introduction   13

Chapter 1
Invest in Valuable Relationships   19

Chapter 2
Value People as God Does   37

Chapter 3
Endure Hardship   49

Chapter 4
Discipline your life   61

Chapter 5
Finish the Race   79

Epilogue   97

Introduction

When I (Kirimi) was growing up, there was a song in our language that went like: "The day I die I will be very happy to leave this body because the troubles of this world are constantly seeking to deny me eternal life." I remember one of my primary school teachers who swore never to sing that song — perhaps for fear of death. Even at that tender age, his reaction to this song set me thinking hard about life beyond the grave. So many questions were triggered in my mind: Why was he afraid of death? What would happen if one died? How is it that the memories of some people who died a while ago are still fresh in our minds, yet there are others who died recently but have faded from our memory? What would people remember me for?

I believe it's the desire of every human being to make a difference in their lifetime, whether in the church, at the work place, or in the home. But the question is, what legacy will you leave as you exit this world? What would be the correct epitaph on your grave when you die? Will you be known for having been the wisest, richest or most educated man of your time?

I often find myself teaching, preaching, or training people and any time I get to ask the participants whether any would like to leave a legacy, I get the full house raising their hands to indicate they would. However, when I seek to know who has put in place a mechanism to ensure they will leave a legacy, I get little response, sometimes none.

In an exercise in one of my leadership classes, I remember asking the students to pause for a moment, close their eyes and reflect on their lives. The next step in the exercise proved harder for them as I sought to know from each one of them what value they have added in this world, and for which they could be remembered if their lives came to an abrupt end. This exercise proved even more difficult because my students were Africans; in the African tradition it is a taboo to ponder on your own death. No wonder a majority of us die without a written will for fear of addressing the issue of death.

The aim of the challenge that I put to the class, however, was not to focus on death but the significance of our lives here on earth. The book of Hebrews 9:27 reminds us that we all have an appointment with death. One thing is sure for each person who is alive (including you who is reading this book!), you have an appointment with death. And it is the Creator who alone knows the time of the appointment. It is therefore imperative that each one of us lives each day with eternity in mind and with the desire to leave a worthy legacy. The question is, will you have lived your life to the fullest when the time of leaving comes?

As a matter of fact, the book of Ecclesiastes reminds us that there is a time for every purpose under heaven, a time to be born, and a time to die. This affirms the fact that death is certain as long as we are alive.

A friend of mine classifies people who are alive into two categories – those who do so much with their lives that when they die it is difficult to know what to omit in their eulogy; and those do so little with their lives that it is hard to find what to say about them. Needless to say, it is worthwhile to find out into which category your life can be classified.

More often than not, when we are confronted with the question of what contribution we are making in society, we find excuses in resources and many other things. But we fail to remember that "to whom much is given, much is expected," and just like in the Parable of the Talents, the person who received five talents and the one who got two talents received the same commendation: "Well done, good, and faithful servant, you have been faithful over a few things, I will make you ruler over many things; Enter into the joy of your Lord." What was important was that they had multiplied their talents. To the one who had not been faithful with the talent, the judgement was fearful: "And cast the unprofitable servant into the outer darkness. There will be weeping and gnashing of teeth" (Matthew 25:30, NKJV).

In his sermon "The Solitary Life", Dr James Allan in 1926 demonstrated that we can leave a legacy despite our limitations in life. He used the life of Jesus to prove his point.

One Solitary Life

He was born in an obscure village
The child of a peasant woman
He grew up in another obscure village
Where he worked in a carpenter shop
Until he was thirty

He never wrote a book
He never held an office
He never went to college
He never visited a big city
He never travelled more than two hundred miles
From the place where he was born
He did none of the things
Usually associated with greatness
He had no credentials but himself

He was only thirty three

His friends ran away
One of them denied him
He was turned over to his enemies
And went through the mockery of a trial
He was nailed to a cross between two thieves
While dying, his executioners gambled for his clothing
The only property he had on earth

When he was dead

He was laid in a borrowed grave

Through the pity of a friend

Nineteen centuries have come and gone

And today Jesus is the central figure of the human race

And the leader of mankind's progress

All the armies that have ever marched

All the navies that have ever sailed

All the parliaments that have ever sat

All the kings that ever reigned put together

Have not affected the life of mankind on earth

As powerfully as that one solitary life[1]

Jesus Christ is our great example. With limited resources, he managed to leave an unmatched legacy. I am confident that no one else will match this legacy.

In his book *Building Your Leadership Resume*, Pastor Johnny Hunt wrote the following: "When my life is over and my legacy written, I don't want to be someone who was almost what God had called him to be."[2] I know that you share that same resolve — to be used for great purposes, to effect lasting change, to have an impact on future generations so that your influence doesn't dry up and blow away at your death.

For you to leave a legacy, you need to live your life well, embracing principles that go with the kind of life that is fruitful and worthy emulating. Those are some of the principles I share in this book and which, if lived out, will assure you a legacy worthy of leaving after your life on this earth is over.

Chapter 1

Invest in Valuable Relationships

...Love the Lord your God with all your
heart and with all your soul and with all your
strength and with all your mind, and love the
your neighbour as yourself.
Luke 9:27 (NIV)

O ne of the wonders of our times are the skyscrapers that are found in many cities of the world today. Men have built very tall buildings. The secret of these buildings is in their foundation. If you desire to build a strong building, then the foundation must be right, or else the building comes tumbling down.

Jesus used the parable of the builder in Luke 6:46-49 to illustrate the need to build on solid foundation.

> *Why do you call me, 'Lord, Lord,' and do not do what I say? I will show you what he is like who comes to me and hears my words and puts them into practice. He is like a man building a house, who dug down deep and laid the foundation on rock. When a flood came, the torrent struck that house but could not shake it, because it was well built. But the one who hears my words and does not put them into practice is like a man who built a house on the ground without a foundation. The moment the torrent struck that house, it collapsed and its destruction was complete.*

If the foundation of our relationships is not solid, when the floods and storms of life come our way, great will be the fall. In the same manner, we will leave a legacy if we lay the right foundation. A life that promises a good legacy is characterized by the ability to develop strong and valuable relationships.

The free dictionary by Farlex defines "relationship" as "the condition or fact of being **related**; connection or association, a particular type of connection existing between people related to or having dealings with each other."[3] Relationship involves two or more people. Relationship involves friendship of two parties who care about each other. In order for their relationship to grow and develop well, they have to know each other well, spending quality time with each other. The other prerequisite is for both parties to respect each other and be willing to serve and sacrifice for each other. In any meaningful relationship, each party must be willing to give and to take.

Often, people in relationships go to the extent of obtaining things that help them remember their relationship: spouses, for instance, share rings and gifts. In the business world, partners sign agreements that set forth conditions of their relationship. Examples of relationships go on and on and we cannot exhaust the different ways in which the parties involved maintain them.

In the Bible, God has shown clearly how we are to go about having valuable relationships. A good example can be seen at the very beginning when God created man. Genesis Chapter Two is a detailed account of how God facilitated life in the Garden of Eden, culminating in giving Adam a wife to help where animals could not. Moreover, according to Chapter 3 verse 8, God would come to fellowship with this couple in person. What a good example God gives when it comes to cultivating a relationship!

Jesus engaged in much public debate with the Pharisees and Sadducees, two religious factions that opposed Him and his teachings. It was during one of these debates that He revealed the greatest commandment. The account in Mark 12:28-31 tells us how one of the teachers of the Law (a lawyer) came and heard them debating. Noticing that Jesus had given them a good answer, he asked him, "Of all the commandments, which is the most important?"

"The most important one," answered Jesus, is this: 'Hear, O Israel, the Lord our God, the Lord is one. Love the Lord your God with all your heart and with all your soul and with all your mind and with all your strength.' The second is this: 'Love your neighbour as yourself.' There is no commandment greater than these."

Jesus added a second commandment that one ought to love their neighbour as himself or herself. Then he explained that every other law of God hinged on these two laws. What did he mean by that? If you love God, would you ignore him or speak badly about him? If you love your neighbour, will you steal from him or hurt him? No! The other laws (don't steal, don't take the Lord's name in vain, etc) all are an amplification of the law on loving God and loving man.

Simply put, the commandments to love God and man embodied the Old Testament law and the teaching of the prophets. If we were to categorize each of the 613 do's and don'ts (as per the rabbis' count), they would come under either "loving God" or "loving our fellow man." This is even clearer in the Ten Commandments. Moreover, while in a sense loving God, our fellow men, and ourselves seem separate activities, they are also interconnected. You really can't do one effectively without doing the other.

As a matter of fact, John amplified the commandment of love thus:

> *If we say we love God, but hate others, we are liars. For we cannot love God, whom we have not seen, if we do not love others, whom we have seen (1 John 4:20, TEV).*

All human responsibility can be categorized into three areas:

1. **Relationship with God (vertical relationship).** God is our creator and we have a duty to worship Him. This is our religious responsibility, an act of love that should come deep from inside us as individuals.

2. **Relationship with both our family members and our neighbours (horizontal relationship).** We have an obligation to our fellow human beings, the first duty given us by God, who created all men "in His own image." The fact that people are created in God's image makes them exceedingly important and hence worthy of respect and love.

3. **Relationship with self.** The third responsibility, not stated but implied, is to self. It comes after the first and second

obligations: since you also are made in God's image, you qualify to love yourself. Really, it is by loving yourself that you enhance your capacity to love others.

1. Relationship with God

The Nature of Love

Love is one word that is used quite often. Preachers preach about it; young men and women pursue it; and even the worst sinners seek it. But what is love? A common dictionary describes it as "an intense feeling of deep affection." It is also expressed through romance and could culminate in sex. According to the dictionary, the word is also used to describe those things that we like very much or in which we find pleasure. However, this popular usage of the word doesn't capture Jesus' meaning when He said that loving God and loving your fellow man are the greatest of all God's commandments, a summary of the law and the prophets.

> *Hearing that Jesus had silenced the Sadducees, the Pharisees got together. One of them, an expert in the law, tested him with this question: "Teacher, which is the greatest commandment in the Law?" Jesus replied: " 'Love the Lord your God with all your heart and with all your soul and with all your mind. This is the first and greatest commandment. And the second is like it: 'Love your neighbour as yourself. All the Law and the Prophets hang on these two commandments (Matthew 22:34-40).*

The Bible never uses the word "love" in some of the senses in which we use it today. The Greek language, in which the New Testament was written, did have the word *phileo*, which refers to the type of love that involves **"feelings, instinct, and warm affection."** This is the love we have for family, friends, and brethren.

But the Greek equivalent of the "love" we will focus on here is *agape*. This love has been described as the love of the intellect, involving a disposition that is characterized by devotion to the object of this love. This kind of love doesn't so much emanate from emotion as from a calculated determination.

Whereas *phileo* describes love's feelings or emotions, *agape* speaks of love's actions. These aspects of love may exist simultaneously, but often there are times, by our actions, when we demonstrate love to those for whom we feel no warm attachment or emotional connection. God is Holy (1 Peter 1:16) and has the most repugnance for sin. Yet according to Romans 5:8, He loved us while we were yet sinners, even to send His only begotten Son Jesus to come and die for us. God acted in love when our condition called for anything but love, and He commanded us to love in like manner. We are to love our enemies, including those who despitefully use and persecute us (Matthew 5:44). It is doubtful that we can have warm emotional feelings for our enemies, but we will have expressed love by being good to them the way God did to us when we were yet in sin.

How Do We Love God?

Certainly when we consider what God by sacrificing His only son did for us, we ought to be affected emotionally. But loving God is more than a warm feeling or affection. Someone has written that loving God is a way of life, a devoted commitment that affects one's very existence. The apostle Paul seemed to speak in this vein when he said, *"For me to live is Christ"* (Philippians 1:23).

Since God is not visible with our eyes (Colossians 1:15), our love for Him is guided by Scriptures. We demonstrate our love for God by obeying His Word. Indeed Jesus the Son of God and hence God manifested in the flesh told his disciples, *"If you love Me, keep My commandments"* (John 14:15). In his letter, John wrote: *"Whoever claims to live in him [Jesus] must walk as Jesus did"* (1 John 2:6). Obeying God's commands enables us to imitate Him, worship Him with our whole being, and to love Him. And if we imitate Him, we will not find it hard to demonstrate love for others. John in his exhortation summed it up this way: *"Beloved, let us love one another, for love is of God; and everyone who loves is born of God and knows God. He who does not love does not know God, for God is love"* (1 John 4:7-8).

Again, love for God is not a mushy, superficial emotion. It is not merely expressed by waving our hands over our heads and chanting "Jesus, Jesus, Jesus" or the like. Love for God is a serious dedication to emulate Him. His Word reveals what He considers righteous and unrighteous. By obeying, we conform to and partake of His divine nature (2 Peter 1:2-9).

What else do we know about God's Love?

- It is not partial or limited, but universal. God loves all people: *"For God so loved the world that he gave his one and only Son, that whoever believes in him shall not perish but have eternal life"* (John 3:16). That doesn't mean He won't punish the wicked, but His sacrifice of Jesus demonstrates God's unwillingness to see anyone lost. *"The Lord is not slow in keeping his promise, as some understand slowness. He is patient with you, not wanting anyone to perish, but everyone to come to repentance"* (2 Peter 3:9).

- His love is not merely felt; it is concretely demonstrated through action. We see it as real and not as an abstraction.

- God's love is unselfish. *"Let this mind be in you which was also in Christ Jesus, Who, being in the form of God, did not consider it robbery to be equal with God, but made Himself of no reputation, taking the form of a bondservant, and coming in the likeness of men. And being found in appearance as a man, He humbled Himself and became obedient to the point of death, even the death of the cross"* (Philippians 2:5-8).

- Words fail in expressing the magnitude of this love. *"Thanks be to God for His indescribable gift"* (2 Corinthians 9:15). It is also unquenchable (Romans 8:31-39).

Therefore, when we love God, we love learning His ways by

studying His Word. And we seek to be like Him and have Him living within us.

There are lessons we can learn from Jesus about his relationship with God:

- **The relationship was certain** – Jesus was sure of his relationship with the Father as evident from what he said, *"If you really knew me, you would know my Father as well. From now on, you do know him and have seen him."* Philip said, *"Lord, show us the Father and that will be enough for us."* Jesus answered: *"Don't you know me, Philip, even after I have been among you such a long time? Anyone who has seen me has seen the Father. How can you say, 'Show us the Father'? Don't you believe that I am in the Father, and that the Father is in me? The words I say to you are not just my own. Rather, it is the Father, living in me, who is doing his work"* (John 14:7-10).

  "I and the Father are one" (John 10:30).

  "I am the true vine, and my Father is the gardener" (John 15:1).

  Are you certain that you have a relationship with God?

- **Jesus lived to do the will of His father** (those things that would make his Father happy): *"All that the Father gives me will come to me, and whoever comes to me I will never drive away. For I have come down from heaven not to do my will but to do the* *will of him who sent me. And this is the will of him who sent me that I shall lose none of all that he has given me, but raise them up at the last day. For my Father's will is that everyone who looks to the Son and believes in him shall have eternal life, and I will raise him up at the last day"* (John 6:37-40).

Is your focus on things that make your Father in heaven proud or do you major on what makes Him sad to the extent of regretting creating you as He did in the days of Noah (Genesis 6:6)?

- **Jesus was very intentional about spending time with his Father from a very tender age**. When his parents traced him in the temple after searching for him, thinking he was lost, he responded to them by asking, *"Why were you searching for me? Didn't you know I had to be in my Father's house?"* (Luke 2:49).

How intentional are you in spending time with your Father or in your heavenly Father's business?

2. Relationship with family and friends

Our obligation to fellow human beings is a charge from God, who created people "in His own image". Being created in God's image qualifies people to be respected and loved.

Jesus set an example for us to follow:

- He invested time with his disciples, whom he referred to as friends in John 15:13-15: *Greater love has no one than this, that he lay down his life for his friends. You are my friends if you do what I command. I no longer call you servants, because a servant does not know his master's business. Instead, I have called you friends, for everything that I learned from my Father I have made known to you.*

- He attended the wedding at Cana of Galilee.

- His friendship with the family of Lazarus, Mary and Martha is clearly evident when he refers to Lazarus as ' our friend' as he addressed his disciples in John 11:11: *After he had said this, he went on to tell them, 'Our friend Lazarus has fallen asleep; but I am going there to wake him up'.*

Indeed Jesus commanded us to love one another; according to John 13, it is through love that the world would know that we are his disciples.

There are lessons we can learn from the life of Jesus so far as the love for family and friends is concerned:

- **Jesus was available for his family and friends**. It's difficult to develop a relationship with people who are unavailable. Jesus accompanied his family to a wedding in Cana where he performed his first miracle. He accompanied his friends for boat rides and even shared meals often with them. Are you available for your family and friends? Can your family and friends depend on you when they need you?

- **Jesus identified with friends in times of need.** When Lazarus died, Jesus visited with Mary and Martha and even wept with them. The world we live in is full of turmoil. As a matter of fact Jesus told his disciples that in this world they would experience trouble but encouraged them to be of good cheer, as he had overcome the world. Do you identify with family and friends when they are in need?

- **Jesus was part of a solution, not a problem, to his family and friends.** At the wedding in Cana, he provided wine. At Mary and Martha's home he raised Lazarus from the dead, turning mourning into dancing and increasing the faith of many who were present. Do you seek to provide solutions for challenges facing family and friends, or do you contribute to making the going tougher for them?

- **Jesus prayed for his family and friends.** There is a record of Jesus praying for Peter in Luke 22:31-31, for his disciples in John 17:6-19, and for all believers in John 17:20-26. Jesus understood the only true and tested way to influence family and friends – praying for them – and set an example by doing just that. How often do you pray for your family and friends?

- **Jesus was open and truthful in dealing with his friends**. He shared his plans with them, putting them in the picture of what was about to happen. He intimated to his disciples about his coming death and resurrection and, as a result, taught and prepared them. How open and truthful are you with your friends?

- **Jesus served his family and friends** (John13:1-17). He washed his disciples' feet, even Judas who would later betray him. The greatest challenge to our relationships is how to serve those who have betrayed us, yet we have a command from Jesus to love our enemies and pray for them. *"But I tell you: Love your enemies and pray for those who persecute you"* (Matthew 5:44).

I came across these words by Dr. Kent M. Keith that I thought summarize what to expect as you serve both family and friends:

People are unreasonable, illogical and self-centred.
Love them anyway.
If you do good, people will accuse you of
selfish ulterior motives.
Do good anyway.

If you are successful, you win false friends
and true enemies.
Succeed anyway.

The good you do today will be forgotten tomorrow.
Do good anyway.

Honesty and frankness make you vulnerable.
Be honest and frank anyway.

What you spend years building may
be destroyed overnight.
Build anyway.

People really need help but may attack
you if you help them.
Help people anyway.

Give the world the best you have and
you'll get kicked in the teeth.
Give the world the best you've got anyway.

- **Jesus forgave and let go**: We, too, need to learn to forgive
  and let go. At the cross Jesus prayed, *"Forgive them father..."*
  One thing I have learnt is that when I don't forgive, I carry
  the burden of unforgiveness myself and also risk not being
  forgiven. This awareness has greatly helped me. Have you
  learnt to forgive and let go when people hurt you?

3. Relationship with self

The third responsibility, not stated but implied, is to self. It
comes after our first and second obligations. Since you too are made
in God's image, you are to love yourself.

34

When you love yourself, you enhance your ability to extend love to others. In John 17:1-5 Jesus prayed for himself first. The supplications he offered after this on behalf of the disciples are remarkable.

When you have a relationship with yourself, then you will be concerned about what you do, what you eat and drink, as these are the foundations of a physically, spiritually and socially healthy you! All this is covered in greater detail in the chapter on self-discipline.

Jesus had a healthy relationship with himself. That is why he knew when to do what. Indeed there are times he left his friends and associates to take a rest in a lonely place.

Developing valuable relationships is necessary in our quest to understand the purpose of life. Life can be lonely and frustrating if one fails to understand and develop valuable relationships.

Prayer:

Dear heavenly Father,

I know that relationships are hard to build and demanding to sustain, yet it is very rewarding to maintain healthy relationships. Give me the strength and energy to develop a meaningful relationship with You, my family and neighbours and even with myself. When distractions come my way, help me to remember that they are just distractions and not lose focus on what you have called me to do. I thank you for this day!

In Jesus' name I pray,

Amen.

Action Steps

_____

_____

_____

_____

Chapter 2

Value People as God Does

Greater love hath no man than this that a
man lay down his life for his friends.
John 15:13

When I (Kirimi) was growing up, my mother loved to tell me stories. A memorable one she told me is about a man who was very rich. In addition to his riches, he was so kind that whenever any family in his village had a calamity, he always sent financial assistance, though he never appeared in person.

One day, as fate would have it, his wife died. His fellow villagers decided to reciprocate his kindness — but only in monetary terms! And so the man found himself with all the money that he needed but no one from the village to comfort him or assist him with the funeral arrangements. That is when he learnt that money cannot take the place of people. People mean more than money.

It's necessary to know that money is not everything in life. Yet it's surprising how far people go as they look for it. Many will lie, kill, name it, for the sake of money, yet they will not go to similar extent for other more important things of life. Below is how an anonymous writer compared money to other things – including relationships – that we invariably take for granted.

Money can buy you a house but not a home
Money can buy you a bed but not sleep
Money can buy you medicine but not health
Money can buy you blood but not life
Money can buy you a girl but not love
Money can buy you amusement but not happiness
Money can buy you books but not wisdom
Money can buy you a clock but not more time
Money can buy you companions but not friends

Money can buy you food but not appetite
Money can buy you a ring but not a marriage[5]

In today's world we are conditioned to equating success with driving a big car, owning property, among symbols of opulence. Such a narrow view of success reduces us to a people who worship material things, a people who are spiritually and socially bankrupt. That is not to say that material wealth is bad. We need money to finance our daily needs like buying groceries, mortgage, children's education, utility bills, etc. In fact, genuine spirituality culminates in material wealth, since it is God who makes people rich. A certain amount of material wealth is necessary unless you live in Mars or Venus. A person who is unable to pay his debt, for instance, has a problem reaching the people he owes money for Jesus. The problem with material wealth lies in human nature which is characterized by insatiable desire for more, better and bigger things. People without strong moral values will trade their integrity for more and more. Cases of lawyers misappropriating clients' funds and doctors prescribing drugs to patients without due care abound as often reported in the media. Generally, people in these professions are among the best paid, yet they still give in to the human nature of greed that has brought about the suffering of many.

In the African culture, people were more valued than anything else. It is sad that modernity is beginning to upset our values and priorities. Whereas in the African culture people were viewed as a resource worthy of sustenance, the perspective today is completely the opposite. In the African culture, skills were passed on to the next generation through a careful process of selection and development, which emphasized intensive investment in people. The same case applies to the African culture, which was handed down through a select few who were initiated as repositories of folklore.

According to the Scriptures, God's love for mankind was demonstrated by His investment in sending His only begotten Son Jesus to die on the cross so that the relationship He had with man before the appearance of sin could be restored. God invested in reconciling us to himself so that we may in turn invest in reconciling others to Him. Paul had this to say to the Corinthians: *All this is from God, who reconciled us to himself through Christ and gave us the ministry of reconciliation: that God was reconciling the world to himself in Christ, not counting men's sins against them. And he has committed to us the message of reconciliation* (2 Corinthians 5:18-19).

Jesus taught and demonstrated his love for people and importance to invest in them when he said:

> *"This is my commandment, that ye love one*
> *another, as I have loved you. Greater love hath*
> *no man than this that a man lay down his life*
> *for his friends" (John 15:12-13).*

According to this passage of Scripture, the ultimate demonstration of love is by a person dying for his or her friends the way Jesus did. We are also instructed to love one another as Christ loved us. He loved us to the extent of laying down His life for us through His ministry, death and resurrection, He was living for us.

One of the great thinkers of the past (I don't remember his name) said that it takes as much courage to live for your friends as it does to die for them. It would require courage to die for friends, even when that courage is motivated by love. However, as good as dying for a friend is, I believe that living for a friend is just as important. By dying for a friend, you prove your love with the ultimate sacrifice, blood.

Living for a friend is being committed to him or her. The Saviour's life models true friendship: perfect love, commitment to teach by word and deed, readiness to mourn with those who are mourning, willingness to give support, etc.

The spirit of love is evident from the first page of the New Testament to the last. Jesus taught everyone. He counted his twelve apostles among his dearest friends. When they came back after being sent out and they complained that they couldn't cast out certain evil spirits, Christ was patient to teach them what to do for a more successful ministry.

Jesus was committed to his disciples and to the work of salvation that he had come on earth to do. He was tireless in his ministry, going to great length to serve, even washing the apostles' feet. He made time to be with his friends and mourned with them as well. Even when Jesus wanted to be alone and the multitudes came to him, he did not selfishly insist on relaxing; he went on to teach them. By this, Jesus demonstrated remarkable love and commitment to serve.

If we were to have such an attitude towards friends, then we could have a lasting impact on them. Isn't that what true Christianity is all about?

Dying or living for our friends is a testimony of our love for them. If they begin to sense that love, then we will have succeeded.

There are many times when our Christianity has been tested. I have repeatedly told my friends that the world is no longer looking for professing Christians but for Christians who are living out what they profess. On the morning I (Kirimi) was writing about the need to live and die for our friends, I received a call that a close friend had gone to be with the Lord. I had so much planned for the day, one of them being to fine tune and present the last chapter of this book to the editor. My ability to practice that which I teach others was being tested and I had to put off the things I had planned for the day to, among other things, rush and help take the body to the mortuary and pray with the family of my departed friend.

According to the book of James, true religion is practical. There has been so much emphasis on the relationship with God, which I totally agree. However, that relationship should compel us to be more practical in our faith by investing in people – and particularly those who are most vulnerable in the society we live in, the widows and orphans.

> *"This is pure and undefiled religion in the sight of our God and Father, to visit orphans and widows in their distress, and to keep oneself unspotted by the world" (James 1:27).*

Another example from the Scriptures on the need to invest in people is the transfer of leadership from Elijah to Elisha. Elisha had been training under Elijah for 10 years. He had seen God deliver His people and deal with the idol worshippers by the hand of Elijah. He had seen the faithful helped and the unfaithful perish. Now it was time for Elijah to die and Elisha to take over. This was a tough moment, for sure. It was time for Elisha to step up and walk in Elijah's shoes; the former was about to lose his mentor and master. Even though there were believers remaining in Israel, the king of Israel was evil (most of them were) and the prophet's responsibility of correcting a people bent on doing evil continually was daunting. But Elisha took the mantle.

Apostle Paul invested in Timothy. Although Timothy was a timid young man who was naturally shy, Paul saw in him potential and made him an understudy and as they served together in the gospel. Over time, a relationship developed between them that Paul in Philippians 12:22 compares to that of a son and his father. Timothy travelled with Paul and the former continued some of Paul's work of overseeing churches when Paul could not physically manage to do it. Both benefited from the relationship! Paul had the delight of seeing a young man mature into a courageous servant of God, a 'son' with whom to share his vision and continue his work. Through the relationship, Timothy acquired a 'father' who never gave up on him but taught and instructed him on how to live life in the Lord. He had a mentor who practised what he preached in every way and lived a life that the young man desired to emulate. *"Whatever you have learned or received or heard from me [Paul], or seen in me, put it into practice"* (Phil 4:9).

Each of us needs to invest in three kinds of people, a Paul, a Barnabas and a Timothy: a Paul, an older man who can build into your life; a Barnabas, a soul brother to whom you can be accountable; and a Timothy, a younger man into whose life you are building.

Moses' investment in Joshua's life demonstrates how one can be a powerful influence in another man's life. Moses spent time with Joshua and eventually the latter became a man of God like Moses. Moses' relationship with Joshua produced a great leader who led the nation of Israel during the challenging period of entering the Promised Land.

John Mark probably knew Jesus when the former was a child or a youth, even though Mark was not a disciple then. The Upper Room where the disciples often met in Jerusalem may have been a room in the house of Mark's family.

Mark accompanied Paul and Barnabas on their first missionary journey. Later, Mark became Peter's assistant. We believe that the account he wrote of Jesus' life and teachings after the deaths of Peter and Paul was based mostly on Peter's teaching rather than on Mark's own personal experience.

From these examples, we establish that we leave a legacy by investing in people, as a result of which our ministry lasts longer than our lifetime. Other lessons we can learn from these examples are:

- Investing in people is a slow process which takes time. It is not something that can be done and accomplished in a few months.

- Investing in people requires commitment.

- We have to have confidence in people's abilities and empower them to do even better than we may have done.

- We need to be selective in the people that we invest in so that we can ensure that they will be good stewards of the investment we have made in them.

Prayer:

Dear heavenly Father,

I know that investing in people is challenging and demanding, yet this is the only way to leave a lasting legacy. Help me to identify faithful stewards in whom to invest, for the glory and honour of your name. I pray for strength for those who are in the process of investing in others.

I thank you for this day. In Jesus' name I do pray.

Amen.

Action Steps

_____

_____

_____

_____

Chapter 3

Endure
Hardship

"Man born of woman is of few days and full
of trouble" (Job 14:1).

◆ ⇒◆✳◆⇐ ◆

"I have told you these things, so that in
me you may have peace. In this world you
will have trouble. But take heart! I have
overcome the world"
(John 16:33).

When I (Stephen) was a child, I looked forward to growing up and overcome the challenges that I was facing at the time. When I became a teenager, I realized that I was up against greater challenges than when I was a child. Then I became an adult and as I write this chapter, I can tell you I am surrounded by greater challenges than those which I had contended with when I was a young person. The challenges I face today are not to do with my personal life alone. They include decisions that I make about my ministry, my family and many others; they are certainly more complex than any I have encountered before in my life.

Possibly it's such challenges that made an anonymous writer pen the following words in an email entitled, "I Quit."

My Resignation

I am hereby officially tendering my resignation as an adult. I have decided I would like to accept the responsibilities of an 8 year old again.

I want to go to McDonald's and think that it is a four star restaurant.

I want to sail sticks across a fresh mud puddle, skid rocks across the mill pond and make a sidewalk with rocks.

I want to roller skate and play ball in the street, play 'Rover Red Rover', 'Hide and Seek' and ride my iron wheel wagon down the hill.

I want to think M&Ms are better than money because you can eat them.

I want to lie under a big oak tree and run a lemonade stand with my friends on a hot summer's day.

I want to return to a time when life was simple. When all I knew were colors, most of my multiplication tables, and a few nursery rhymes. All I knew was to be happy and I was blissfully unaware of all the things that should make me worried or upset.

I want to sleep in a tent in the back yard without worry or fear.

I want to think the world is fair. That everyone is honest and good.

I want to believe anything is possible.

I want to be oblivious to the complexities of life and be overly excited by the little things again.

I want to live simple again. I don't want my day to consist of computer crashes, mountains of paperwork, depressing news, how to survive more days in the month than there is money in the bank, doctor's bills, gossip, illness, and the loss of loved ones.

I want to believe in the power of smiles, hugs, kind words, truth, justice, peace, dreams, imagination, mankind, and making angels in the snow.

So here is my check book and my car keys, my credit card bills and all my statements. I am officially resigning from adulthood.

And if you want to discuss this further, you'll have to catch me first, cause...

TAG! YOU'RE IT! See Later... Alligator[6]

When one's survival is threatened, he or she can swim in the deepest ocean or climb the highest peak.

It is a fact that life is full of challenges. None of us can claim not to have challenges in life. The word "challenge" means to make a call or summons, to engage in a contest, to be something that by nature or character serves as a call to battle, contest in a special effort.

Challenges approached with the right perspective can help one achieve hitherto impossible feats.

The way we look at challenges of life determines how we act and the results we get from our lives. Based on the definition of what challenge is according to this chapter, we can remember many people who have given up because of different challenges in their lives. By way of substantiation, I hereby present a few challenges that I have faced and the results that I have seen them produce.

During my (Stephen) early school days, most students in my school were from poor families and life was very hard for us. Our parents had a hard time raising school fees. It was not uncommon to see a child stay at home for a half or a whole school term for lack of fees. Then after the fees were paid, one would go back to school and continue where he or she had left off. During that time of waiting for fees, many lost hope and, frustrated by the interruption to their education, looked for something else to do. But some of us persevered and instead of viewing this waiting negatively decided that no matter what it takes, we would continue with our education until we realized our dreams of life. The challenge was great, the situation embarrassing and frustrating, but by making up our minds to face it and putting our trust in the Lord, we prevailed. Our patience and resolve helped us to get through it all, and that is why we are where we are now.

I am a witness that God is faithful and that He rewards those who trust in Him. The Bible says that those who trust in the Lord will do exploits. A wise person somewhere once said: "The difference between a failure and a successful person is that a successful person doesn't quit." None of us is a failure. People choose to fail the same way they choose to succeed; dealing with challenges positively is the way we refuse to be failures. Also by viewing challenges as catalysts to our destiny. The Bible is called Good News because it contains good news for mankind, that we are to have dominion over everything else that God has created. *"Then God said, let us make man in our image, according to our likeness let them have dominion over the fish of the sea, the cattle, over all thing that creeps on the earth"* (Genesis 1: 26).

Whenever a gadget is manufactured, the manufacturer makes sure that he provides a manual for operating it. In the same way, God had a plan in creating us, and His plan is for us to live a meaningful (or abundant) life. It is therefore imperative that we read the manual of our Manufacturer, the Lord God, to know how to manage ourselves for a life with a meaning. God created us in His image and His plan is for us to function in a way that makes us have dominion over the earth. And we can only understand the real picture of what dominion is through a brief exegesis of the word.

The word "dominion" means complete and absolute authority or ownership or a sphere of knowledge, influence or control. The fact that the word means that I am complete means that I lack nothing and have all it takes to deal with my challenges.

Friends, we must go back to the original plan and take our authoritative position in life. I don't know about you, but whenever I read that I was created to have dominion, my heart rejoices because I get imbued with fresh assurance that I have the key to unlock my destiny. The awareness that people were created to have dominion is a prerequisite for all those who want to overcome mediocrity. Jesus said to Peter, "I am giving you the key and whatever you bind on earth is bound in heaven and whatever you loose on earth will be loosed in heaven" (Mathew 18:18). We are to take the authority that is given to the saints and deal with every challenge. We were created to be victors, not victims. We were created to be conquerors, not to be conquered by challenges of life. My prayer to anyone who reads this book is that you will discover the real you and the fact that you were created with power in you. Yes, I mean unlocked potential that has never been realized and which, if fully exploited, will turn around your circumstances.

Greater is He that is in us than the one that is in the world. You are wired with solutions to problems, and the spirit of fear should not immobilize your life. Jesus told his disciples to be sober and vigilant because the enemy, the devil, walks about like a roaring lion seeking whom to devour (I Peter 5:8). It must have been the same revelation that prompted David to write Psalms 23. The enemy will be there, and sometimes you will suffer to the point of sensing the shadow of death, but it is always good to look beyond the challenges. David testifies that in times of his challenges he knew that the protection of God was there to take him through. Moreover, he saw, in times of challenges, a table in the presence of his enemies. A table is a symbol of victory, signifying celebration.

The third thing that encouraged David was the fact that the goodness and mercy of God was sure to follow him. Whenever I read Psalms 23 verse 6, I am reminded that the goodness of God comes with protection and provision to those who will endure in times of challenges. Nor is this goodness a one-time thing; it continues all the days of the believer's life. 1 Peter 5:7 is a reminder that challenges from the devil are temporary. One, the devil boasts of power that he actually doesn't have. The verse says that the devil walks about like a roaring lion. That tells me that the enemy can only attack if given a chance. It is a fact that every one of us, both Christians and non-Christians, has an enemy. Although unseen by the natural eye, this adversary is not imaginary. This enemy is a real person, a spirit being with intelligence and known characteristics, whose goal is to steal, kill, and destroy (John 10:10). And whether you realize it or not, the enemy has targeted you as a victim. All the time the devil is planning how to bring you down. His work is to kill and to destroy. But all is not lost; we have One who overcomes all the challenges and schemes of the devil, and His goal is to give us life in its fullness, the Lord God. That's why you cannot afford to live a defeated life. It's time to wake up and remind the enemy that you are more than a conqueror!

The enemy's schemes of hindering people from a victorious life are generally covert in nature. He disguises his activities in people's lives through all sorts of methods, including inspiring temptations and all manner of evil thoughts. Other times he tries to shift your focus from the real problems so that you keep blaming other people rather than taking responsibility of your life. Overcoming this enemy starts with the acknowledgement of one's depravity and helplessness, and then seeking power from God to do whatever you cannot do on your own.

Here are some biblical insights that can help you to deal with the enemy

- The challenges of life are not greater than our God. The Bible shows that in the beginning God created heaven and earth. All that is in the world exists by His authority. The maker of heaven and earth has authority over the challenges of life. The Bible says that what is impossible with man is possible with God (Luke 18:27). Even as you read this book, remember that you did not get it by accident; it was brought your way by God in His divine plan. It is time you realized that God has many victories for you, one of which is to help you overcome the challenges that are standing in your way today. My prayer is that you get the revelation to recognize the power of God and what He is about to do in your life today.

- The perspective that you have of your challenges will determine whether you become victorious or get overcome. The action you are going to take today after reading this book will either open a new dispensation for you or ensure that you continue marking time, saddled to your oppressive circumstances. It is good to listen to the voice of the Lord and follow His command. In the book of Exodus we are told of the twelve spies who were sent to spy the Promised Land. When they came back, ten of them gave a negative report of how and why it was not possible to cross over to Canaan. They had seen giants and claimed that compared to their enemies, they looked like grasshoppers. Their perspective of the challenges was they were helpless before the Canaanites. But in the same group there were two people, Joshua and Caleb, who did not agree with the other ten. Their perspective was completely different. Instead of focusing on the challenges, they focused on the promises of God. They understood who their God is and what He is able to do for them. (Numbers 13:1-14,9). Of those who left Egypt, these two are the only ones who reached the Promised Land. The rest were children of those who died in the wilderness.

- When facing challenges, avoid negative views from negative people.

- Remember that you were created to solve problems no matter how difficult they look.

- If challenges are not confronted, they do not necessarily go; they enslave you.

- Challenges are not there to wipe us out but to propel us to our destiny.

- When facing challenges in life, remember there is power in the Word of God. The book of Proverbs exhorts us not to forget the teaching of the Word of God but to keep it in our hearts so as to live long (Proverbs 3:1).

- When facing challenges, you should not lean on your own understanding (Proverbs 3:5); the Bible requires you to trust in the Lord with all our heart.

Prayer:

Dear heavenly Father,

I thank you for overcoming the world and assuring me to be victorious too through faith in You. Give me the strength to overcome the many challenges the enemy has brought my way. You have destined me to be an overcomer and I know that I have overcome with Your strength. I believe I can do all things through Christ who strengthens me. I thank You for this day!

In Jesus name I pray

Amen

Action Steps

_____

_____

_____

_____

Chapter 4

Discipline
Your Life

He that hath no rule over his own spirit is
like a city that is broken down,
and without walls.
Proverbs 25:28

I (Kirimi) remember my days as a high school teacher when students dreaded their appointment with the discipline master. But whereas the students dreaded the visit because it ended in pain inflicted on them, the discipline master was actually helping them harmonize their behaviour with the expectations of the school and their desire to succeed. And generally that's what disciple does – to bring order in our lives.

Discipline is:

- A way of inculcating knowledge or learning

- A way of enforcing obedience (putting one's body in subjection to do God's will)

- Temperance/self-control and orderly conduct (results of discipline)

- Deliberate submission to authority and control to God and others.

We often think of discipline as punishment—but it is much more. Did you know that the words "disciple" and "discipline" have the same root word, which means to learn? As disciples of Jesus Christ, we must be disciplined, that is, learners.

Dr. Phil Pringle wrote: "Discipline sticks to the plan once we are underway, no matter what problems, obstacles or feelings we face.

Discipline lives by principle rather than by emotion. Discipline does what is right even when we don't feel like doing it. Discipline keeps going, even when we are discouraged, have lost faith, or are facing seemingly impossible odds. Discipline is the making of character: indiscipline is the unmaking of character. Discipline creates a habit, a way of life, a lifestyle."

Following are some of the reasons why we need to discipline ourselves:

- So that we do not become castaways, salt without savour: Apostle Paul says, *"But I keep under my body, and bring it into subjection: lest that by any means, when I have preached to others, I myself should be a castaway"* (I Corinthians 9:27).

- So that we do not bring reproach to the name of Christ: *"For the name of God is blasphemed among the Gentiles through you, as it is written"* (Romans 2:24).

- To protect ourselves from the enemy: *"He that hath no rule over his own spirit is like a city that is broken down, and without walls"* (Proverbs 25:28).

- To understand what it means to submit to God and authority: *"Obey them that have the rule over you, and submit yourselves: for they watch for your souls, as they that must give account, that they may do it with joy, and not with grief: for that is unprofitable for you"* (Hebrews 13:17).

"Submit yourselves to every ordinance of man for the Lord's sake"(1 Peter 2:13).

"Likewise, ye younger people, submit yourselves unto the elder. Yea, all of you be subject one to another, and be clothed with humility: for God resisteth the proud, and giveth grace to the humble" (1 Peter 5:5).

- So that we live victoriously: *"He openeth also their ear to discipline, and commandeth that they return from iniquity. If they obey and serve him, they shall spend their days in prosperity, and their years in pleasures. But if they obey not, they shall perish by the sword, and they shall die without knowledge"* (Job 36:10-12).

- So that we do not distract others. *"If eating meat will make my brother to stumble, then I will never again eat meat, lest I make my brother stumble* (1 Corinthians 8:13).

- To prepare ourselves for times of testing and suffering. When we learn to seek the presence of God through discipline in calm times, we are able to get into His presence in difficult times too.

In the old days, a city was fortified using a thick stone wall built around it. In the absence of these walls, invaders could come and go at will, ravaging the city and its inhabitants. When a person lacks discipline, he or she is comparable to a city without walls and hence without protection. In that state, Satan and all manner of foul spirits are free to invade one's life as they please. (Remember when Jesus called Peter "Satan" in the book of Matthew?) Many Christians are walking around defeated, and this is because they lack discipline to obey God and resist sin. They are like a city that is broken down.

People are always looking for a solution to their spiritual powerlessness. But I've got it! Read the Bible, obey the Bible, seek God's face through prayer! Once this becomes part of you, it will not be long before you begin to see the Lord move in your life.

It's not a surprise to hear Christians talking about needing some therapy for sin. This is one of the most ridiculous concepts. You don't need therapy; you need forgiveness and discipline to seek Jesus and stop sinning. If your problem is overeating, say no to the chow and go pray. Paul said some good stuff about disciplining/self-control:

> *"All things are lawful unto me, but all things are not expedient: all things are lawful for me, but I will not be brought under the power of any"* (1 Corinthians 6:12).

Did you notice the emphasis? He said, "I will not be brought under the power of any." You too can say it out loud right now. I will not be brought under the power of television! I will not be brought under the power of work! I will not be brought under the power of sin! I WILL subject myself under the power of God. In Jesus' name, Amen.

Paul also said:

> *"But I keep under my body, and bring it into subjection: lest that by any means, when I have preached to others, I myself should be a castaway"(I Corinthians 9:27).*

Your inner man ought to dictate what the outer man should do as the Holy Ghost guides you. You have a part to play in your relationship with God. Yet God is not asking you to do anything grievous like cutting your hand off! If you love Him, all he is asking of you is to read His Word and obey it. The Scriptures say that that is your reasonable service – to offer yourself as a living sacrifice by obeying His Word (Romans 12:1).

In a world of irresponsible freedom, there are several areas of our lives that should be brought under discipline:

I. Your Flesh

Paul reveals in I Corinthians 9:27 that he kept his body under discipline. Let's consider, for example, the sin of adultery.

How and why do Christians get involved in adultery? The reason is that they do not discipline themselves by saying yes to God's guidance and help everyday. Some days, by their actions, they say, I don't need you today, Lord. I can handle this. Notice I said, "some days." Christians don't just jump into an adulterous relationship; they ignore early warning signs from the Spirit of God. Think about David watching Bathsheba bathing from his balcony. He knew he shouldn't have been doing that, but he continued. In the end he got her pregnant and ended up killing her husband. The consequences were bitter. Apart from the fact the child born in this sinful relationship died, the sword never left the household of David.

Paul, writing to Titus in Titus 2:3-4, says that the elder women are to teach the younger women. I Timothy 5:2 says men are to treat the older women as mothers and the younger women as sisters, with all purity. Victory over the flesh comes by walking in the Spirit, which requires that you discipline yourself to listen to and obey the Word of God, the Bible. "Walk in the Spirit, and ye shall not fulfil the lust of the flesh (Galatians 5:16).

II. Your Mind

Our minds have a great capacity, yet the same capacity can be used for good or evil. When God created man, He gave him the ability to choose. One of the choices we have to make is to fill our minds with those things that are good. Paul exhorts the Philippians to think on those things that are true, noble, right, pure, lovely and admirable (Philippians 4:8).

The writer of Proverbs tells us: *For as he [a person] thinketh in his heart, so is he: Eat and drink, saith he to thee; but his heart is not with thee* (Proverbs 23:7).

Paul's advice to the Roman church is very crucial to us: *Do not conform any longer to the pattern of this world, but be transformed by the renewing of your mind. Then you will be able to test and approve what God's will is—his good, pleasing and perfect will* (Romans 12:2).

Your attitude should be the same as that of Christ Jesus (Phil 2:5).

It is important to discipline our minds. Remember that what we feed our minds on is what will come out in form of words and deeds. Indeed the Bible reminds us that out of the abundance of the heart, the mouth speaks.

Dr. Pringle wrote: "The shape of our mind is the shape of our lives. When we fail to discipline our thoughts, we default to a negative mindset. We have to set our minds on the right course. Our mind, like an unattended garden, grows weeds choking out good plants. We can cultivate our minds by reading great books, having great speakers, meditating on beautiful things, speaking and writing things that demand the best thinking."

III. Your Eyes

There is a saying among the Swahili people of Kenya that the eyes have no curtains. Though we may try to convince ourselves that we can look at everything and get away with it, experience has always proved us wrong. Nor is anyone who insists on looking at the wrong things safe as is evident in King David's issue with Bathsheba. That is why Job's statement comes in handy:

"I made a covenant with my eyes not to look lustfully at a girl" (Job 31:1).

We ought to make a covenant with our eyes concerning what television program to watch, what website page to visit and what not to feast our eyes on, as the eyes are the gateway to our minds.

IV. Your Ears

The book of Proverbs is full of wisdom for living. In Proverbs 18:15, the NAS version puts it this way: "The mind of the prudent acquires knowledge, **And the ear of the wise seeks knowledge.**"

You are to deliberately choose to make your ears listen to only those things that will increase your knowledge. Needless to say, gossiping, backbiting and tearing others down are not part of what adds knowledge.

V. Your Mouth

James had this to say concerning the tongue: *"But no man can tame the tongue. It is a restless evil, full of deadly poison"* (James 3:8).

It is important that you discipline your mouth. Watch out for instance, some jokes that you may crack and leave many laughing but someone hurt. It is important, too, that you discipline your mouth not to tell a lie, a thing that often happens when one is seeking acceptance in a group.

> *"We all stumble in many ways. If anyone is never at fault in what he says, he is a perfect man, able to keep his whole body in check"*
> *(James 3:2).*

In his book, *"Top 10 Qualities of Great Leaders"*, Dr. Pringle wrote that the mouth is powerful. It's like a loaded gun, a stick of dynamite, a canon, a bent bow and arrow, a sword, a trowel, a pen, a pouring river. He adds that all these items can be good or bad, builders or destroyers, creators of life or bringers of death. It depends on the user.[7]

It is in the light of this awareness that the advice by the preacher in Ecclesiastes becomes very meaningful:

> *There is a time to tear and a time to mend, a*
> *time to be silent and a time to speak, ...*
> *(Ecclesiastes 3:7).*

There are moments when keeping silent is best for us. We do not have to contribute to every discussion. If we did so, we are likely to reveal our ignorance. As Dr. Pringle says, if we don't know a lot about the subject being talked about, the less we say the better, since it's time to learn.

At the same time, watch for what you eat. Paul is clearly against the brethren who knowingly eat food offered to idols, particularly if doing so will cause a weak brother to stumble.

VI. **Accountability**. Many people go through life without making an effort to account for their actions. No wonder such people do not accomplish much. Whether it's in the work place, church or even family, we need to be accountable so that we can remain focused on our goals. Imagine a work situation where you are not required to work for a particular number of hours, reporting only when you feel like showing up. Very little would be achieved. Life is the same. If we are not accountable, chances are that we won't accomplish much or leave a legacy. Interestingly enough, this trend of lack of transparency is creeping into the church as well. There are many believers who will not commit themselves to a given church, constantly hopping from one congregation to another. Experience shows that such people never accomplish much to leave a legacy.

There are some important thoughts that I need to share with you:

- If you are a teacher, you have an even greater responsibility to discipline yourself.

> *Thou therefore which teachest another, teachest thou not thyself? (Romans 2:21a).*

How can you teach something that you do not know personally? Jesus declared the Pharisees to be blind leaders of the blind; and of course when the blind lead the blind, both shall fall into the ditch. Dear teacher, don't take your students down with you; discipline yourself! This applies to any kind of teaching, formal or informal.

- **Rein in your will**

If you have a Bible in your house, don't ask God to make you read it. Just pick it up and read it. You may want to ask God to give you increased desire to read. That's alright, but don't ask Him to make you read it; that is up to you. You've got to make the decision to read. I know that you are sometimes tired or strongly drawn to your favourite TV show, but you ought to purposely create time for the studying of God's Word.

If you won't read the Word, you won't grow and bear the fruit you should. And when you stand before the Judgment Seat of Christ to give account of what you've done as a Christian, you'll be ashamed for not having done anything. It will be a moment of shame, especially considering what the righteous One did for you.

- **Examine Your Life Daily**

When you see yourself slipping, get back on track—fast! Our natural tendency is to rationalize our behaviour. When God tells you something isn't right, don't overrule what He is saying to you. Make haste to make amends.

• **Be a Strong City, Built Up and Fortified**

Don't live a spiritually powerless life. God can do for you what He did for His people of old. James reminds us:

> *Elias [Elijah] was a man subject to like passions as we are (James 5:17).*

Yet that man, Elijah, was mighty in deed by God's grace. He submitted himself to the Lord. You too were made to be a strong spiritual giant. Read the Bible to familiarize yourself with the mighty men and women of God and their exploits. These people were mighty because they believed God and did what He said. It is no different today. Believe God and do what He says and you too will be what God created you to be: built up and rooted in His Son Jesus Christ.

Let's stop blubbering about our problems but become examples to other believers and the world of charity, peace, and spiritual might. Christ overcame this old man and declared you an overcomer because of what he did on the cross.

It is imperative that we be

- Disciplined in making a conscious decision to love the Lord every day

- Disciplined in making a conscious decision to love our neighbour every day

- Disciplined in making sure we read the Bible every day

- Disciplined in listening and obeying the Holy Ghost's prompting/unction

- Disciplined in making sure we obey God's statutes and commands every day

- Disciplined to resist sin every second

- Disciplined in praying for others and self

- Disciplined in using our spiritual gifts

- Disciplined in serving Christ in our ministries

- Disciplined in fasting regularly.

In order to become a strong, mature Christian, you must exercise discipline in these areas; otherwise, a lukewarm Christian life results, characterized by all the guilty feelings that come with wilful disobedience.

We should discipline our lives to focus on the things that are important and that's why the advice from the gospel according to St. Matthew is very crucial:

> *But seek first his kingdom and his righteousness,*
> *and all these things will be given to you as well*
> *(Matthew 6:33).*

Prayer:

Dear Heavenly Father,

Discipline is one of the things that we ordinarily wish away, yet this is what is needed for us to finish the race well and get the commendation "Well done, you good and faithful servant." I desire to finish well and I ask for grace to discipline myself in all areas. I thank you because you set an example for me to follow. I thank You for this day and the opportunity to live for you!

In Jesus Name I pray,

Amen.

Action Steps

_____

_____

_____

_____

Chapter 5

Finish the Race

"Therefore we also, since we are surrounded
by so great a cloud of witnesses, let us lay
aside every weight, and the sin which so easily
ensnares us, and let us run with endurance
the race that is set before us"
Hebrews 12:1

I'd like to take your mind back to October 20, 1968 in Mexico City's Olympic Stadium. The time, 7.00 pm. The closing ceremony had just been completed. The spectators and athletes, still warm from the euphoria of the celebration, were gathering their belongings to leave the stadium. Then the announcer asked them to remain in their seats. Down the boulevard came the whine of police sirens. From their vantage point, many in the stadium could see motorcycles with their flashing blue lights, encircling someone making his way toward the stadium. Whoever it was, he was moving slowly. Everyone remained seated to see the last chapter of the Olympics take place.

By the time the police escort got to the stadium, the public address announcer said that a final marathoner would be making his way into the arena and around the track to the finish line. Confusion was evident among the crowd. The last marathoner had come in hours ago. The medals had already been awarded. What had taken this man so long? But the first sign of the runner making his way out of the tunnel and onto the track told the whole story. John Stephen Akhwari from Tanzania, covered with blood, hobbled into the light. He had taken a horrible fall early in the race, whacked his head, damaged his knee, and endured a trampling before he could get back on his feet. And there he was, over 40 kilometres later, stumbling his way to the finish line. The response of the crowd was so overwhelming, it was almost frightening. They encouraged Akhwari through the last few meters of his race with a thundering ovation that far exceeded the one given the man who, hours earlier, had come in first. When Akhwari crossed the finish line, he collapsed into the arms of the medical personnel who immediately whisked him off to the hospital.

The next day, Akhwari appeared before sports journalists to field their questions about his extraordinary feat. The first question was the one any of us would have asked, "Why, after sustaining the kinds of injuries you did, would you ever get up and proceed to the finish line when there was no way you could possibly place in the race?" John Stephen Akhwari answered: "My country did not send me over 7,000 miles to start a race. They sent me to finish it."

I personally started my spiritual race when I invited Jesus into my heart. I do not know when I will cross the finish line. But I am determined to finish and do it on a high note. I have fixed my eyes on Jesus, my Saviour, best friend, encourager, coach and Lord.

FINISH THE RACE!

> *Brothers, I do not consider myself yet to have taken hold of it. But one thing I do: Forgetting what is behind and straining toward what is ahead, I press on toward the goal to win the prize for which God has called me heavenward in Christ Jesus (Philippians 3:13).*

It is clear that Paul was keen on one thing: pressing on toward the goal to win the prize. Moreover, two key things are highlighted in this verse:

I.   First, Paul reveals his resolve to **forget what is behind.**
Our past can become the biggest obstacle to our future, be
it failure, sin, name it. For Paul, his past included murder.
Don't you think that Satan sometimes tried to discourage
Paul by reminding him of his past? Satan will seek to use
your past, too, to discourage you.

II.   Second, Paul makes us aware that he kept **straining toward
what is ahead.** Victorious Christian living is not a leisure
walk in the park. The word apostle Paul uses to describe the
scenario – "straining"— suggests active struggle. There is
effort involved, a battle filled with moments when you think,
"It would be easier to quit."

People are remembered for how they finish, whether it is their
lives, their relationships or their ministry. When the going gets
tough, God helps us run the race before us.

When Vincent Foster, Deputy White House Counsel, committed
suicide in 1993, Clinton said, "It would be wrong to define a life like
Vincent Foster's in terms only of how it ended." Nonetheless, that's
how Foster will be remembered—by how he finished the race. The
end of a life—or anything else—defines all that went before it.

The writer of the book of Hebrews does not only write about
running the race but also finishing it well.

*Therefore, since we are surrounded by such a
great cloud of witnesses, let us throw off everything that hinders and the sin that so easily en-
tangles, and let us run with perseverance the race
marked out for us. Let us fix our eyes on Jesus,
the author and perfecter of our faith, who for
the joy set before him endured the cross, scorning
its shame, and sat down at the right hand of the
throne of God. Consider him who endured such
opposition from sinful men, so that you will not
grow weary and lose heart (Hebrews 12:1-3).*

I remember the running competitions when I was in school. The track was well marked and each runner had to keep to their own track. The inner track always seemed like a better deal than the outer one but that was only perception.

Runners couldn't cut corners to shorten the race. They had to run the race marked out for them. It's the same in the Christian life. Someone else's race might seem easier than your own, but God says, *I want you to run this race. Don't think about others.* You have your race cut out for you!

If you're going to finish, you've got to keep running until you reach the finish line. As we have seen earlier concerning the 1968 Olympics, hours after the marathon winner crossed the finish line, Tanzania's John Stephen Akhwari limped across the finish line, injured in a fall early in the race. Asked why he didn't quit, he said, "My country did not send me 7,000 miles to start this race. My country sent me to finish it." So it is with God. He didn't just commission us to start the race. He wanted us to start and finish it. Sometimes the race is filled with pain, but God will help us finish it, and finish it strong!

The Boston Marathon's Heartbreak Hill, at mile 19, tests runners to the core. It is life's long, steep hills, like the one in the Boston Marathon, that really test our faith and trust in the Lord. We should persevere through "Heartbreak Hill" and continue on until we get to the finish line.

According to James 1:12, "Blessed is the man who perseveres under trial..." At the 1992 Olympics, Derek Redmond tore a hamstring early in the 400-meter race, collapsing. He then got up and limped toward the finish line. His father barrelled out of the stands and cheered his son to the end. Our heavenly Father does so for us too in our spiritual race.

How do you get to finish well?

I. Recognize That You Have Not Arrived Yet

Paul not only recognized that the Lord had a grand purpose for his life, he also realized that he had not arrived as long as he was in this world. Paul knew he is not what he should be. He was aware of his faults and the areas where he still needed to grow. The Greek word for "perfect" also means "complete". Paul recognized that he had not finished the race yet as long as he was in this world. Chuck Swindoll says it well: "God is seeking progress, not perfection."

Please hear this. Some people get so discouraged because they feel they aren't progressing rapidly. The Christian life is a life of growth and maturity . . . much like life itself. Growth takes time. As diligently as Paul worked at his faith, he still had not arrived. Don't get discouraged . . . keep moving forward. Growth takes time.

Some people have a different problem. They have concluded that they have "arrived" at where God wants them to be. They have reached a certain point in their knowledge or experience and they assume that they are mature and can stop working so hard. But those who think so have a faulty view of their own situation. They are looking only at the surface, God is concerned with the heart.

We must evaluate ourselves by Christ. He wants us to be pure in our actions, in our conversations, in our thinking, in our attitudes, in our relationships. He wants us to love Him more than anything else. He wants to be in the position of influence in every part of our life. If you understand what is expected of you, you will, like Paul, understand that you are not there yet.

II. Don't Live In The Past

Paul shows us that if we want to grow, we must "forget" the past. Obviously Paul is not telling us to literally not remember anything. Certainly we should remember who we were before Christ found us. We should remember the times we have seen God's faithfulness demonstrated. We need to remember the mistakes we've made so that we can avoid them in the future.

Paul is not even telling us that we don't have to fulfil the responsibilities of the past. If we have wronged someone, we should try to make amends. If we have stolen from someone, we should make restitution. If we have a problem with someone, we should seek to be reconciled.

When Paul talks about forgetting, he is telling us that we can't, and must not, live in the past. What happened in the past has passed and we must keep going forward. There are two reasons we need to forget the past. First, people have a tendency to <u>fixate on the past</u>. We will hold on to some bad experience and allow it to weigh us down. We will remember a hurt that someone inflicted and it will eat us up. We will remember a time when we stumbled and determine to never try again. But how we deal with the painful times of the past is what determines how we live in the present. We ought to learn from the pain and then move on. The burden God has forgiven should never be taken back again.

Second, we have a tendency to <u>rest on the past</u>. We will replay the past victories and be content to remember them instead of continuing to push ahead. This happens to many people. Paul determined that he would not rest on past accomplishments but always look forward to what was yet undone. There are Christians who are always talking about the victories of the past. They talk about how intimate their relationship with Christ was. But it is all past tense, a past we should forget and focus on the present.

Sports teams have this problem. They get a great victory and then rest in the glory of that victory forgetting to practice. In the next game they end up losing to an inferior opponent because they lost their focus.

III. Be Intentional About Your Growth

Paul tells us that he "presses on". This is the same word that was used in verse 6 when Paul talked about his zealous persecution of the early church. It is with that same kind of zeal that Paul, upon getting converted, pursues God's plan for his life. Paul also says, "this one thing I do". He is single-minded. He is not distracted. He clearly knew where he was headed.

He tells us that he is stretching forward, he is reaching for his goal. He is not only concentrating, he is straining forward. The image conjured up is like that of running in a race. You see people in a race leaning forward to try to beat their opponents to the tape. This is the image Paul uses to communicate his desire to grow spiritually.

It will require persistence

Some of mankind's greatest contributions were made by people who decided that no sacrifice was too large and no effort too great to accomplish what they set out to do. Edward Gibbon spent 26 years writing *The History of the Decline and Fall of the Roman Empire*. Noah Webster worked diligently for 36 years to bring into print the first edition of his dictionary. It is said that the Roman orator Cicero practised before friends every day for 30 years in order to perfect his public speaking. What stamina! What persistence!

We live in a world that requires everything instantly. We have microwaves to warm our food instantly, automated teller machines to dispense money anytime we need it, instant coffee machines. The list is endless.

Now think about how much energy we put into the Lord's work. The comparison can be rather embarrassing. And it should lead us to ask ourselves some heart-searching questions: Why is our service for Christ sometimes performed in a half-hearted manner? Why do other things always come before our time with the Lord? Why do we prepare more diligently for secular work than we do in an effort to serve God better?

Growth will not take place if we do things haphazardly in our spiritual life. Practically, diligence means:

- making time for God in our schedule;

- finding time to thoughtfully read the Bible;

- planning for times of prayer;

- making worship and service a priority in our day to day planning;

- doing a regular and honest spiritual evaluation of our lives;

- turning away from worldly pursuits;

- pushing ourselves to study and read for growth; and

- daring to reach beyond what is always comfortable and safe.

A successful coach reported that he lived by a very simple creed he found one time:

Press on.
Nothing in the world
Can take the place of persistence.

> *Talent will not;*
> *Nothing is more common*
> *Than unsuccessful men*
> *With talent.*
> *Genius will not;*
> *Unrewarded genius*
> *Is almost a proverb.*
> *Education will not;*
> *The world is full of*
> *Educated derelicts.*
> *Persistence and determination*
> *Alone are important.*

IV. Focus On The Goal

Paul realized that he must always keep his eyes on the prize. It is like the Olympic athlete who trains tirelessly for a gold medal at the Olympics. When one gets tired, he or she imagines what it will be like to stand on the platform and hear the national anthem of their country being played in honour of their victory. That picture spurs them on.

Years ago a young black child was growing up in Cleveland, in a home which he later described as "materially poor but spiritually rich."

One day a famous athlete, Charlie Paddock, came to his school to speak to the students. At the time, Paddock was considered "the fastest human being alive." He told the children, "Listen! What do you want to be? You name it and then believe that God will help you be it." That little boy decided that he too wanted to be the fastest human being on earth.

The boy went to his track coach and told him of his new dream. His coach told him, "It's great to have a dream, but to attain your dream, you must build a ladder to it. Here is the ladder to your dream. The first rung is determination! And the second rung is dedication! The third rung is discipline! And the fourth rung is attitude!"

Armed with this discovery, he went on to win four gold medals in the 1936 Berlin Olympics. He won the 100-meter dash and broke the Olympic and world records for the 200 meters. His broad jump record lasted for twenty-four years. His name? Jesse Owens. [James S. Hewett, Illustrations Unlimited (Wheaton: Tyndale House Publishers, Inc, 1988) pp. 26-27.]

So, what is the prize that should spur you on? What image should you keep in the forefront in your mind? I invite you to imagine the following in your mind:

- Seeing yourself standing before the Father, the creator of heaven and earth, and hearing Him say, "Well done thou faithful servant!"

- Seeing your life reviewed with only highlights of victory.

- Seeing yourself surrounded by those whose lives have been redeemed, partly because of your faithful witness.

- Seeing someone describe your life as consistent and as an example of faithfulness during your funeral service.

- Seeing the joy of that moment when you meet Jesus for the first time in heaven.

Many people begin dieting or start exercising but never follow through. Many start reading a book but never finish. Some begin training in an area of endeavour but give up when it becomes difficult. Some get married and opt out at the earliest sign of difficulty. Some people are fascinated by faith in God for a while and then grow bored, moving on to something else that promises excitement. Is that you? Is your faith superficial? Are you a temporary follower, or are you fully committed to Christ?

The person who gives up misses out on the benefit that comes with persisting to the end. The one who leaves a marriage misses out on a quality relationship. The one who gives up on exercising and dieting sacrifices good health. Those who give up on education miss out on the things they could learn. And those who give up the race for the heavenly prize miss out on the joy of walking with Christ.

So, what is the one thing you are focused on? Are you focused on stuff like paying bills, gaining power, pursuing temporary peaks of enjoyment? Don't you want more from life? If you do, set your eyes higher! Press for the prize! Seek to know the Lord better and more fully. Jesus tells us that when we seek first the kingdom of God, he will add to us the other things that we are concerned about.

Maybe you are near the finish line, your earthly life nearing conclusion. Don't coast now! Now is the time to "kick" so as to finish strong. Maybe you are just getting started, having known the Lord recently. Don't give up because the going is getting hard. Keep working; be patient. Growth takes time. Maybe you are right in the heat of the race. Don't relax your effort. Keep pushing. I know it is exhausting at times, but focus on the goal! Strive to finish well.

Paul is encouraging us to be more than names on a church roll. He doesn't want us to merely call ourselves Christians or just think of ourselves as Christians. He wants us to seek to know Christ and be conformed to his suffering, since Jesus our role model didn't give up either. May God help you and I in pursuing this noble desire.

Like Paul, towards the end of his life, we want to be able to say, "I have fought the good fight, *I have finished the race, I have kept the faith*" (2 Timothy 4:7).

Prayer:

Dear Heavenly Father,

I am aware that finishing a race can sometimes be challenging. Also as any runner knows, I am aware it is very rewarding once you cross the finish line. Father, give me the strength and energy to persevere to the end. I pray to know when hindrances come my way, and to remember that they are only distractions that seek to move my focus from what You have called me to do. I thank You for this day!

In Jesus name I pray.

Amen.

Action Steps

_____

_____

_____

_____

Epilogue

Then I heard a voice from heaven say, "Write:
Blessed are the dead who die in the Lord
from now on." "Yes," says the Spirit, "they
will rest from their labor, for their deeds will
follow them."
Revelation 14:13

In his book *What Are You Living For? Investing Your Life in What Matters Most*, Pat Williams identifies four false and meaningless and four true and satisfying reasons for living. The false reasons for living are:

1. **Fortune** – There are people to whom money is the meaning of life. They see their lives as a competitive game and their bank account is the scoreboard. The more their net worth grows, the farther ahead they are in the game of life. Yet it is apparent that with all the money accumulated, it will not do you any good on the day you draw your final breath.

2. **Fame** – There are people to whom fame is the meaning of life. They derive their status and self-worth from being recognized and applauded. A lot of people seek to have everybody know their names and envy their position in life.

3. **Power** – There are people to whom power is the meaning of life and think that wielding power will give them meaning and satisfaction in life. They are always striving to attain power and control over others, to control circumstances, to have a total mastery over their own lives.

4. **Pleasure** – There are those who think they can substitute pleasure for meaning in life. Pleasure takes many forms: the lust for sex, or fine food, or luxury, or entertainment. If it feels good, do it! If it tastes good, eat it! If you want it, buy it!

But, the four true and satisfying reasons for living and worth dying for are:

1. **Character** – God wants to shape us and make us like Him. He wants our character to be like His character. The more we seek to pattern our lives after God and after His son, Jesus, the more we achieve His goal and purpose for our lives.

2. **Influence** – Our influence is the impact we have on the lives of others. Instead of living only for ourseleves, God wants us to live for others and to pass on to the next generation our best traits, values, beliefs and dreams for the future. Through our influence, the very best part of us lives on even after we physically die.

3. **Parenting** – This is the process of raising another generation to carry on our faith, values and meaningful traditions. It includes any form of guiding, discipling, training, leading, encouraging and affirming of young people, whether we are biologically related to them or not.

4. **Faith** – Our faith is about what we believe in, and it's the most important reason ofor living.

Aware that our lives have eternal significance, these four reasons ought to give purpose for living. The good we have done continues on, even after our dying breath. Most important of all is to know that our existence doesn't end; the life God intended for us to experience from the beginning of time is just beginning.

Dr. Pringle wrote, "Our lives are our legacy. Great leaders live lives worth remembering and worth modelling ourselves on. The life of Jesus Christ continues to be the greatest life ever lived, and his death the greatest death, for by his life and death, he provided a way for millions upon millions to follow, which continues to be the case throughout the world today. He has become the captain of our salvation, the apostle of our faith, the greatest leader of all the time."

Remember, the life we live here on earth will determine a great deal the kind of legacy we leave in this world!

NOTES

1. Allan, J., "One Solitary Life" (1926), http://www.changinglivesonline.org/solitary-life.html (accessed September 25, 2009)

2. Hunt, J. M. *Building Your Leadership Resume,* (B&H Publishing group, 2009) Nashville, Tennessee

3. http://www.thefreedictionary.com/relationship

4. Keith, K.M, *"The Paradoxical Commandments"* http://www.paradoxicalpeople.com/paradoxicalpeople/paradoxical_commandments/(Accessed October 2, 2009)

5. http://www.sikhee.com/whatmoneycanbuyyou.htm

6. http://www.jaredstory.com/resignation.html

7. Pringle, P. *Top 10 Qualities of a Great Leader,* (Harrison House Publishers, 2007) Tulsa, Ok

8. Williams, P. & Denney, J. *What Are You Living For? Investing Your Life in What Matters Most,* (Regal Books, 2008) Ventura, California

About the Authors

Kirimi Barine is the leader of a successful publishing company in Nairobi, Kenya. He is also an author, trainer and consultant,

 as well as an adjunct faculty member of Pan Africa Christian University. In addition, he serves as a leader in his church, social and professional groups.

He holds a Bachelor of Education degree, a Masters in Business Administration from Egerton and Kenyatta universities respectively, and he is currently enrolled for a doctorate degree in Business Administration.

He is a resident of Nairobi, Kenya, together with his wife, Joyce, and their two sons, Alvin and Adrian.

Rev Stephen Barine is an ordained church minister at Crossroads Fellowship Church in Raleigh, North Carolina, where he is in charge of the African Ministry. He is also the current President of International Church Alliance (ICA) an inter-denominational ministry of different African ministers in the USA. Rev Barine and his wife, Mary, have their own counselling practice-Bamyline Family Services Inc., where they practice as licensed professional counsellors.

He holds a Bachelor of Biblical Studies and a Masters degree in counselling from Southeastern Baptist theological Seminary, in Wake Forest, North Carolina.

He is a resident of Wake Forest, North Carolina together with his wife, Mary, and their three children, Kiama, Kawira and Kwendwa Barine.

LaVergne, TN USA
09 February 2010
172570LV00004B/44/P